See Where We Come From!

A First Book of Family Heritage

Scot Ritchie

Kids Can Press

To old and new traditions, and thank you, Margaret and Morgan.

With special thanks to Katherine Ritchie, Nancy Khalil, Eliane Bastos Chiavegatti and Nancy Turner for reviewing this book.

Published in Canada and the U.S. by Kids Can Press Ltd.
25 Dockside Drive, Toronto, ON M5A 0B5

Kids Can Press is a Corus Entertainment Inc. company

www.kidscanpress.com

The artwork in this book was rendered digitally.
The text is set in Futura.

The image of the totem pole that appears on page 25 is based on a hand-painted and carved Haida totem pole.

Edited by Jennifer Stokes
Designed by Michael Reis

Printed and bound in Malaysia in 10/2020
by Tien Wah Press (Pte.) Ltd.

CM 21 0 9 8 7 6 5 4 3 2 1

MIX
Paper from
responsible sources
FSC
www.fsc.org   FSC® C012700

Library and Archives Canada Cataloguing in Publication

Title: See where we come from! : a first book of family heritage / Scot Ritchie.
Names: Ritchie, Scot, author, illustrator.
Series: Ritchie, Scot. Exploring our community.
Description: Series statement: Exploring our community
Identifiers: Canadiana 20200237268 | ISBN 9781525304972 (hardcover)
Subjects: LCSH: Culture — Juvenile literature. | LCSH: Manners and customs — Juvenile literature. | LCSH: Families — Juvenile literature.
Classification: LCC GN357.R58 2021 | DDC j360 — dc23

Kids Can Press gratefully acknowledges that the land on which our office is located is the traditional territory of many nations, including the Mississaugas of the Credit, the Anishnabeg, the Chippewa, the Haudenosaunee and the Wendat peoples and is now home to many diverse First Nations, Inuit and Métis peoples.

We thank the Government of Ontario, through Ontario Creates; the Ontario Arts Council; the Canada Council for the Arts; and the Government of Canada for supporting our publishing activity.

Contents

Show and Celebrate!

Today is a big day for the five friends! This evening, their class is hosting a Heritage Festival. They're going to celebrate the customs and traditions of people all over the world. Each classmate will bring two things to the festival that represent their family heritage: a favorite food and something for show-and-tell.

Martin, Sally, Pedro, Nick and Yulee are best friends, and they each have their own heritage. Did your parents, grandparents or great-grandparents come from somewhere else? Were _you_ born somewhere else? Or have you and your ancestors always lived on the same land?

Pedro's house

Play Music!

Martin's cousin, Taeko, is visiting from Japan, and she and her family are coming to the festival. Taeko brought Martin a special gift.

"In Japan, we call this a shakuhachi," says Taeko.

Music is a tradition that is often handed down from generation to generation. Many cultures celebrate and even tell stories through music or dance.

A shakuhachi [SHA-koo-ha-chee] is a flute made of bamboo.

I can teach you how to play. My dad taught me.

I'll take it to the festival for show-and-tell!

Delicious Dishes!

Martin's mom was born in Japan, and his dad's family is from India. They are preparing food for the festival — one Japanese dish and one Indian dish.

"Udon is my favorite!" says Martin.

"Panipuri is *my* favorite," says Martin's dad.

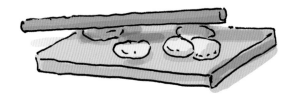

Does anyone in your family prepare special dishes that you love to eat? Preparing and eating traditional foods is a fun — and yummy! — way to learn about your heritage.

Udon [OO-don] is a thick noodle usually made of wheat. It's served with a broth and different toppings, such as tofu, vegetables or fish.

Panipuri [paw-nee-PU-ree] is a crispy fried dough ball with a variety of fillings, such as potato or chutney.

My mom makes udon, too!

Together in the World

Martin can't wait for his friends to meet his cousin. She can tell them all about what it's like to live in Japan. The friends are going to walk to the festival together, and Martin and Taeko's first stop will be Sally's house.

Sharing our heritage can give us a sense of togetherness and belonging. We learn the many ways we are alike, and also what makes us unique.

Tasty Traditions

Sally is excited to meet someone from the other side of the world! She is Haida, and her family's history goes back thousands of years. The Haida are Indigenous Peoples from islands called Haida Gwaii off the northwest coast of Canada and off the southern coast of Alaska. They are part of Sally's heritage.

Learning family traditions, such as food preparation, can help you connect with your family. And one day, you can pass on those traditions to the next generation!

Make Your Own Way

For show-and-tell, Sally is bringing a cedar bark basket. It was made by her grandmother. The things we make and the way we make them can be traditions that are handed down from generation to generation.

Making and wearing traditional crafts and clothing can be a way to show others who you are and what is important to you.

Cedar bark baskets are made by weaving cedar bark.

It's a Goal!

Pedro's house is next. He's wearing his favorite football jersey. Pedro is from Brazil, and football is part of his heritage. He wants to share it with his friends.

"Hey!" exclaims Taeko. "I play on my school's soccer team in Japan!"

In some countries, soccer is called football, but it's the same fun game! People from different parts of the world often play the same sports and games, and sometimes share similar customs and traditions.

16

Part of the Tree

Before they go, Pedro's vovô has something he wants to show the friends. He speaks to them in Portuguese, the official language of Brazil. Pedro translates to English.

"My vovô says that this is our family tree," says Pedro. "The branches show everybody in our family — from many generations ago to today."

A family tree is a way for Pedro to see his past connected to his present. Pedro's family tree shows that even though he and his parents have moved far away, they will always be connected to their relatives in Brazil.

My Family Tree

Grandma
Grandpa
Vovó
Vovô
Mom
Dad
Pedro

Vovó [VO-vah] **means Grandma in Portuguese. Vovô** [VO-voh] **means Grandpa.**

Changing Times

Nick opens his front door wearing his Viking helmet. His ancestors were Scandinavian, from Norway. His moms are making krumkake, Nick's favorite dessert.

"Vikings didn't wear baseball caps," says Nick. "But I'm going to!"

When something is repeated for generations, it can become a tradition. Sometimes we alter parts of our heritage to keep up with changing times. Traditions don't have to stay the same.

Everybody Has a Story

The last stop before the festival is Yulee's apartment. Yulee moved here from Egypt with her grandmother. Her dad still lives and works in Egypt, but he plans to join Yulee soon.

To keep family memories alive, it's important to tell stories. Family stories can help you understand your background, who you are and who you want to be.

Look Around!

Yulee's grandmother packs up the koshary, and off they go! On the way, Sally shows her friends a totem pole. It tells a story of her ancestors.

Seeing special monuments in public spaces lets us know we belong in the bigger community. The marks of different heritages are all around us!

24

Totem poles are wooden carvings of figures and symbols. They are used by Indigenous Peoples of the Pacific Northwest to honor and remember their ancestors, history and beliefs.

Share-and-Tell

The kids place their special items on the table. Pedro shows off his football skills, and the friends take turns playing Martin's shakuhachi. The festival has begun!

There are so many customs and traditions around the world! It's fun to share our own and learn about others in return.

Welcome to All

The food smells so good! The five friends can't wait to eat some of their favorite dishes — and some foods they've never tried before.

Sharing food is a way of sharing our heritage. Some things are familiar and some are new. But respecting other people's customs and beliefs should be part of *everyone's* heritage.

What's Your Story?

Ask your parents and grandparents — and your aunts and uncles! — to tell you their stories. That's the best way to learn about your heritage.

What area of the world do your ancestors come from?

Make a Heritage Box

1. Find a shoebox, hatbox or any other kind of box with a lid.

2. Decorate your box! You can use paint, stencils, stamps, stickers, photographs, fabric, ribbons, beads, buttons or wrapping paper.

Can you see where each of the friends' families are from?

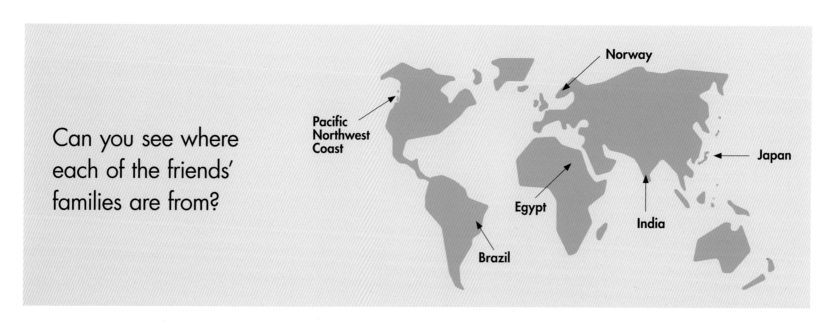

4. Ask your family members to add something special to your box.

3. Fill your box with special items that make you think about your family and its history. You might include a poem or story, a recipe, photographs — and you could even draw your family tree.

Words to Know

ancestors: the people in your family who lived before you

culture: a set of traditions shared by a group of people

custom: a way of doing things that is common to a group of people

family tree: a diagram that shows different generations of a family

generation: a group of people who are born and live around the same time

heritage: traditions and beliefs that are passed down in a family, country or other group

inherit: to receive something that used to belong to someone else

language: words or signs people use to communicate

monument: a structure built to keep alive the memory of a person or event

tradition: the handing down of beliefs and customs, from generation to generation